Aging Grace

The Journey to a Healthy 100

Wellplanet
17201 Primavera Circle
Cape Coral, Fl 33909
(or visit: www.wellplanet.org).

Quotes or references for educational or devotional purposes are encouraged.

Large quantity purchases at volume discounts for study groups at churches or social ministry nonprofit organizations may be given by contacting the Wellplanet community at
www.wellplanet.org
 or www.tomhafer.com

ISBN-*978-0-615-615-59240-4*
Manufactured in the USA
By :Worzalla Publishing Co., Stevens Point, WI

Cover Photo: www.MelindaHawkins.com

Table of Contents

Table of Contents

Dedication

Sara Hafer, my mom. Your untimely death ended your journey before your seventieth birthday. But you lived the full life of many, in three quarter-time. You taught us that life is not the passing of years, but what goes into each day. You will always be our greatest hero, the grandkids will tell stories from generations to come of the woman who taught them unconditional love. On behalf of your entire family, we love and miss you, and know we will reunite someday, when our earthly journey is over.

Ron Patterson, former Volunteers of America, Chief Financial Officer and friend. You seemed to always be the smartest person at any table, as well as one of the most compassionate. The hundreds of ministries that were funded through your 28 years of fiscally responsible stewardship with Volunteers of America continues to reach and uplift two-million lives every year. Your leadership will never be forgotten, and your gentle spirit continues to be felt throughout our great organization in every corner of the nation.

Acknowledgments

Writers might *write* in solitude, but they are never without an army of inspiring people that empower and encourage their effort towards scripting something worthwhile. It takes a village to make a good manuscript.

First and foremost, I would like to thank all the residents at the **Village**, past, present and future. Because of you, there is a story to tell. Secondly, thank you to the almost 350 staff members. Thank you Kevin Ahmadi, for your vision as our captain. And, to the nursing and rehab staff, administration, dining, engineering, and housekeeping, your care continues to be the color that brightens the potentially gray days of the thousands of seniors we are blessed with caring for each year.

For your editing help, thank-you Carolyn McKinney and Sherrie Saidon. For your partnership in reaching the community, thank you Eileyn Sobeck-Bador. To my family - Eileen, Abbey, Dan, and Rachel - you are the greatest! Thanks for all!

Many times we grunt and stumble through life, but yet God allows us to nourish each other, in spite of our occasional clumsiness. We are each a living example of the *wretch* the song refers to. Grace *happens* and God provides nourishment to others through us. And as we age, we get the opportunity to get nostalgic. We dust off the life lessons, sand down the rough parts, and pass them forward to future generations. What an amazing trick. This is *Aging Grace.*

Aging Grace

Thin Place

Diets and exercise lead us to looking and feeling young, attractive, and thin. That is what the magazines say. *Isn't that what it is all about?*

I used to buy health magazines years ago. I stayed current on all the *fad* diets and exercise programs, because that is what I did for a living-that is, I taught people to feel young, attractive, and thin (But, that has all changed. That is not what I do anymore).

Now, I teach people what I have learned from many very smart and very healthy 100 year old people *(Centarian-is the proper term).* The goal of *young, attractive, and thin* will take you forty, or maybe fifty years of life, maybe? The goal of fitness, from the perspective of a deeper *spiritual* awareness, can last 100 years.

The Celtic *(Kel'-tik)* Christians spoke of *Thin Places 1500 years ago.* These were said to be locations at which the separation between one's physical and spiritual worlds were paper thin. To live in a *Thin Place* is to be *aware* that our life journey, although challenging at times, is truly an orchestrated harmonious, God-ordained pilgrimage; a long walk through *Holy Ground*. This spiritual discovery, you will find, is a gift more precious than gold. In fact, besides *eating a healthy diet* and *having meaningful exercise each day*, this awareness could be thought of as the *third* variable that leads towards *one-hundred years* of healthy and inspired living.

I would like to invite you on a spiritual journey....
Imagine... that you are now one-hundred years old today. Imagine that your mind is completely clear and your health is good.

Now, as a *Centarian*, you lean back in your favorite recliner, because you just finished the walk you take every morning. It has been your routine for greater than fifty years.

You close your eyes, your mind starts to drift to yesteryear, to the times you remember as a young person.

In your daydreaming, you think about what your health has meant to you.

As you continue to daydream, you reflect on the natural food you had always consumed. Your diet had always been real, whole foods from the vine, from the branches, directly from the earth. You remember with great fondness, the victory gardens that you planted during the war. You awaken to the fact that, with a little gardening efforts, you always had food provided for you, naturally.

Next, you give thanks for the wonderful community of people that have shared the biggest parts of your life. Somehow, you sense that your motivation for your personal health and wellness, that had lasted one-hundred years, would have never existed if you had no caring community with which you could share your life. It is the *love* of the community that kept you going, kept you alive, and kept you knowing what the Creator had in mind for you to live this way, together in community.

Your "nourishment" is not just from food, but from the love that is received by others. You conclude that your good health is possible because of three basic variables for health: *food, exercise,* and *yes, love!*

You look back on your life and reflect that the best parts of it were *not* when you were *being served*, but those times you were *serving* others. The mission trips to Haiti, the canned food drives, the reading to the kids in Sunday school, the simple walks with the grandkids, sharing stories and laughing. These were the moments that built a long and healthy life.

You discover that the true joy in life came from giving the very best of what you had to offer. That true joy comes from service. The return is tenfold of what *we* give. You discover, that when we include ourselves in the whole community, we take the focus off of *self*. We silence our personal struggle with health and weight-loss when we reach out to others. Living for *self* draws us into battle with the demons of our selfish obsession; but living for others transcends this obsession.

With this understanding and joy, you discover that your efforts towards exercise are no longer seen only as a tool for weight-loss; but, exercise is a life giving gift that allows you to continue your joy in service throughout a long and disability-free life.

Remembering the days of the Great Depression, it becomes hard for you to grasp the current state of the diet and food obsession. Now, so many billions are spent on battling the *curse* of a food *surplus* in our world. You will always see food as a *blessing* from the Creator. You still find it hard to overeat when you remember the members of your community who had nothing.

You often remember the days where there was nothing; so you weep for those who still have no nourishment. And when you weep, you are reminded that you are fully human, capable of great compassion for others. It is empathy that continues to motivate you at one-hundred years old. You hope to help end hunger for others by sharing your abundance.

You find the joy in balancing your supply for it is sharing that you are living in harmony with your neighbor. With this satisfied feeling, there is no need to take more than your share. You find overeating never to be a problem for you.

You also reflect with sadness when you think of all the young people who do not have the luxury of a simpler life that you lived at their age. A life where exercise was a given; because *life* was less sedentary. Jobs were more physical in nature then they are today. And, all the food was natural; free from high fructose corn syrup and added high calorie processing, sodium, and chemicals. As you reflect, you feel sadness for every woman and man who fought the demons of weight-loss and won, then lost, then gained, then lost. You want to help them out of the madness so that they can stand on the solid rock of simple awareness, the same rock where you stand.

You want to teach those who struggle that true freedom comes from belonging to a loving community, serving others. Ultimately, the deeper hunger is satisfied with God, the source of all life, who provides for them with life giving natural healthy foods and the *gift* of movement.

Ultimately, you decide that everyone who currently struggles with obesity, would benefit by knowing what you have discovered as being the basic essentials for living and aging well.

During your reflection, you are aware that there is a practical and simple answer for those who suffer with obesity, type 2 diabetes, heart disease, hypertension, certain types of cancers, and other chronic conditions. You are aware that experts agree that 95% of these chronic conditions are reversible simply through healthy diet and consistent exercise. You also know that there is something much-much deeper that will *fill* the void for so many who are desperately seeking answers to their health problems with no avail.

You decide everyone needs to know these three principles:

First, that everything we need for sustaining health and wellness had been provided for us through nature since the beginning. If not true, life would not be. Today's health crisis is not the fault of the individual, but is a manifestation of our community forgetting our blessings of real, whole, natural foods, and simple life giving water.

Secondly, unlike anything we create by hand, like a car or a refrigerator, which starts to breakdown when used; the body improves in every way with moderate to heavy use. Exercise is a magic pill, a fountain of youth, an anti-depressant; the body is improved in every way possible, naturally with exercise.

And finally, when we care for ourselves to better care for others, our efforts made towards personal fitness become a true spiritual discipline; an expression of gratitude and thanksgiving for all of life.

You are brilliant! But yet, you realize that your clarity did not come from a laboratory nor from a scientific deduction. Your "knowing" came from simple observations over a century and this clarity you possess will bring comfort to all those who suffer needlessly with poor health, and empty hearts. You realize that God provides for us effortlessly through nature. You know that all health problems are improved through exercise; and you also know that healthy living is an expression of gratitude and thanksgiving for life...

And now you awaken from your daydream. Now you are no longer one-hundred years old; but instead you are the age you are right now. And you have the rest of your life to live out in good health, trusting the Creator of the provisions he had given to you naturally.

Brennan Manning, best-selling author and former sought after lecturer and preacher, influenced millions with his writings and retreats for better than 40 years. In his swan-song book that was written with a help of an able friend because Brennan's eyes have grown dim, he is no longer able to function without the patience, love, and *grace* of others. His last book he wrote in his twilight years. It is fitting that he titled it *All is Grace*. In it he writes:

"Over the tar (road) of my life, I have usually been heading toward something along the lines of 'professional commitments' or at least I thought they were. But those trips are over now. I am living in a different emotional direction. I am steering toward home, hardly a poster child for anything...anything, that is, but grace." [i]

I invite you to experience an *aging grace* as you travel the '*tar*' of your life. Discover that your path is truly an orchestrated harmonious God-ordained pilgrimage home. I invite you to discover your personal *Thin Place*, as you explore ours, at the *Village*.

What is Your Story?

I watched an interesting documentary a while back. It was on the life of *screenwriters*. One of the well known writers mentioned that good movies are made all the time, but "great movies" are hard to come by anymore. The documentary pointed out that great movies are hard to come by because so many *hands* are now involved in the process. Instead of a movie going from the writer, to the director, to the actors; giant studios have so much money wrapped up in the process, that they have tables of executives making chops here and there on the writing and production.

Similar to what happens with our foods, the movies gets an *over-processed* version of the initial intention of the story teller. The really-really great stories are not told like it's creator intended for it to be told. Gone are the *Godfathers*, the *Gone with the Winds,* and *It's a Wonderful Life.* Really great masterpieces that were told by great authors, retold by the director's interpretation through the actors, made the masterpieces come alive. It is so often not the case, anymore. The more opinions you have, the more diluted the story. The more the original *flavors* that the creator intended, becomes more and more...vanilla. Most of the time, we experience only a partial representation of what the *Creator* intended for us to see and experience.

This is so true when we think of our own lives. How many opinions do we filter through over the years that instruct us on *what to buy?* Or telling us *How we need to look or act? Whose story are we living? What was the original script for each of our stories, anyway?*

We know that we have unique gifts, talents, and passions. We are *not* one in a million, we are one in seven billion. And, that is just including those alive today. Throughout history, our story never was, until now. And this story will never be told again.

So what is your story?

According to Christians, the greatest story ever told includes the life, death, and resurrection of Jesus. This is the love story of all love stories for the follower of Christianity. Simply, it is the foundation and inspiration that breathes life into all believers' individual stories.

In Judaism, reenacting the Passover Seder meal is retelling the great story of God's love, by remembering the deliverance of Jews from four-hundred years of slavery in Egypt. It is one of many beautiful Jewish stories of God's faithfulness. The story is reenacted so Jews can reconnect and be inspired by the love between God and His faithful people.

Buddha has his story of leaving a life of wealth for a simple life of suffering which eventually led to a rebirth into enlightenment.

All great religious wisdom has this common thread. We start our journey without knowing; we gain the needed wisdom along the path; and, we are delivered from *sin, slavery*, or *suffering* in the process. This is done so beautifully, when we remain still, and let God's story draw us to Him.

It appears that the older one gets, the more profound one's wisdom becomes. The longer one lives out his personal story, the more he potentially illuminates God's story of love for His people. The aging one is the artist, who is painting, writing, or playing out reflections of God's love story for God's people.

Through religious practices, we are all retelling God's love story with as many expressions as there are people. As the years pass, it has been my experience, working as both a physical therapist and also a chaplain with seniors, that there is something *most* beautiful about inner beauty that shines progressively brighter, long after the physical beauty of youth fades.

When we celebrate physical beauty to the degree we do, we have our values slightly skewed. So much is celebrated about the vibrancy of youth, the beauty of youth. But, there is something more vibrant, more reverent, and more beautiful than young physical beauty.

The years slowly steal away strength, endurance, vision, and hearing. If aging is done with *grace*, one starts to rely less and less on the physical, and more and more on the spiritual. The aging one learns to trust the Creator. As Emerson said "All I have seen teaches me to trust the Creator for all I have not seen."

It never fails at a wedding that I am officiating, someone mentions something like, "isn't young love wonderful? So full of potential. Is there anything better?"

I can answer with confidence, Yes! There is something better than young love, full of potential. It is *old* love. Old love is better. Old love that has tested time, through sickness and health, richer or poorer, through the sunshine and through the rain. Love that was challenged, and survived. Love that is patient, kind, that does not boast, that is not arrogant or rude, love that does not rejoice in wrongdoing, but rejoices in the truth.[ii] This is love that is a greater love than young love.

As the physical declines, the spiritual increases. As we grow in faith through the years, we continue to reflect the great love story of our faith, with deeper and deeper expression.

In essence, the physical *self* is improved considerably with proper diet and exercise. But, the spiritual *self* increases exponentially more with the discipline of love. T.S. Eliot said:

"We shall not cease from exploration-and the end of all of our exploring-will be to arrive where we started- and know the place for the first time."

We never stop exploring our spiritual selves, for while the body declines, the spirit soars - it never reaches a limit. We reflect God's love brighter and brighter as we grow in wisdom over the years. As we explore our uniqueness, we will always arrive with a greater understanding at just how distinctively special we really are. We are a divine masterpiece, intended that way by our Creator.

G.K. Chesterton once said "It was not long ago that men sang around a table in chorus. Now one sings alone before a microphone for the absurd reason that he can sing better. At this rate, if this behavior were to continue, only one man will laugh, because he can laugh better than the rest."

Does it not seem to be this way? We let the ones who sing best-sing; the ones who are best at sports-play; and the ones who are pretty-dress up.

But what if we are not great singers? What if we are not great at sports? What if we are not terribly pretty?

Ironically, the majority of us are *pretty* average physically, really. Not particularly great at anything, yet good at some things.

But, making a joyful noise, running to catch a ball, or wearing something nice, has nothing to do with talent or beauty. Singing, playing, and dressing nice are joyful things for all of us. I think the lousier you sing, the more entertaining it is to try. The person who is least likely to be picked for the sports teams, almost always seem to have the best sense of sportsmanship; and the one who is fairly plain in appearance, almost never carries the ego that is sometimes attached to a gifted physical beauty.

Yes, ordinary people seem to often be the most genuine people. Nothing against beautiful, athletic people with sweet voices, most of us are just not one of them. The point is, the *Average Joe* loves to sing, loves to play, and loves to look presentable as well. *Beauty* is more than talented singers, gifted athletes, and pretty people.

One thing I really appreciate about older adults, is the fact that inner beauty has a greater chance of shining through when the *burdening* side of youth's physical beauty and abilities has finally faded. When there is no more pressure to keep up the façade of a younger appearance; we embrace our wrinkles and worry no more of hiding them.

Some of the most beautiful women according to *Vogue* are in their 20s. But, under a different lens, *none* of those youth compare to the *inner*-beauty we have seen in women almost eighty years older.

This is the beauty of the community that I serve as pastor and physical therapist. *The Village* is a deep spiritual *well*. A place where the spiritual and the physical are close at hand. The Village is a *Thin Place* for many.

It is when we finally understand that God loves us, I mean really loves us, that a life can be *lived* fully, without anxiety.

When we accept God's grace, we discover that God loves us where we stand; right here, right now, at the age we are today. And this love has no condition. This love changes us from the inside out. Suddenly, with this new understanding, we are no longer shamed or forced into good behavior. We are 'good' naturally, as an expression of the joy in response to the love that God had shown to us first. With this love that we now have in our hearts, we look for opportunities to serve others. Love, responding to love, changes the world.

When we *age with grace*, we witness signs of this new life everywhere where there was only despair. With grace, we see the person who had addictions, suddenly become clean and sober with this new lease on life. We see the angry father, who used to damage his family with his words, suddenly build-up his spouse and children and not tear them down. We see the neighbor who is actively dying, and we sit by his bedside. Not *only* because we can ease the dying neighbor's suffering, but also, our presence eases our own internal suffering. Our involvement makes us whole. In all instances, the addict, the abuser, and the dying, suffering is diminished by *love*. In all instances, love is the catalyst for the action.

Many times a person comes into a Church, Synagogue, or Temple and says to himself *"I feel like I am not worthy to be here, all these people are religious people. They are so sure of their lives. And I am not sure. I am ashamed. Maybe coming here was a bad idea. I'm sorry I bothered these people with my problems, I should leave."*

When I hear something like this from a visitor, I usually apologize on behalf of the entire community. I assure them that if we give the impression that they are not to be there, then shame on us! We are all a broken people. In fact, those who feel they are not broken, are the ones who are not ready to receive God's unconditional love, because they are not completely honest and open with themselves, yet.

We are all in need of this understanding. And, God, who is boundless in justice and mercy, forgives us. We simply need to *know* that we are in *need* of forgiving.

A free gift of God's unconditional love, God's *Grace*, is only received with open hands. And, when we receive this free gift of understanding that we have a God who loves us without condition; We can go into the world with our arms wide open and be that blessing to others, with the love of God in us.

All things are made new, with love. We reach out, in a hurting world, feeding the poor, clothing the naked, visiting the sick, not because we *have* to, but because we are desperately impassioned to act. We are empowered from the inside out, and we cannot help but to be a blessing to others! We become a player in God's endless grace, when we are bold in our telling of our own unique story.

When we have a deeper sense of the Creator's love, we slow down to find the neighbor in need, as a response to that heightened awareness. We can begin to see each other through the lens God sees us. We start to see each other through the lens of love. We start to sand down the rough edges that might irritate, and we begin to accept our differences. We start to build up each other with dignity and respect.

Through love, we become a community; a *village*, regardless of race, creeds, or beliefs. The dignity we give each other is reborn through love as we see each member in God's image. This is the life in community.

Not long ago, **at the Village**, we lost our oldest resident, Astrid. She died at age 104.

Astrid, was a faithful member of our Village Chapel congregation for years. Although age took her sight and her ability to walk, nothing could take her spirit. Every afternoon, I would walk by while Astrid was sitting in the sun with her younger friend, Fran (at the time, she was one-hundred years old). The two of them always had kind words to share.

Just after Astrid's death, Fran sat alone in the sun after lunch. Astrid's chair was empty. When I went to check on her, she would say "I miss my friend so much." Then, we would exchange a hug and a little mutual sadness.

Fran loved her friend, and felt her loss. But in time, the *grace* of the community restored the peace and comfort for Fran, because the members of the Village lived their stories without hesitation or fear.

At the heart of all of our life stories is the desire to become a blessing to others. It is how we know that we are fully alive.

Becoming Alive

Ten of *us* middle-aged guys flew to Haiti six weeks after the devastating earthquake of 2010. It was the first day that commercial airlines started flying into the country again following the tragedy.

We thought there might be a safety issue about going at that time, but we went anyway.

"Don't worry, we will be safe" we told our families; but we had no idea what we were talking about.

We got off the plane to a sea of locals who had no food or shelter (actually, they never really had food or shelter in the first place, but now they really, *really* did not have food or shelter, because of the mass devastation). We walked out of the tiny airport with twenty very large cardboard boxes filled with medicines, food, and clothing that we had promised to take to the school and missionary, *The Village of Hope,* outside Porte-au-Prince.

The ten of us were pushing our boxes in old shopping carts over the dirt road to our taxi. I am sure you have had bad shopping carts at the grocery store. The cart that had the wheel that was stuck and you have to lean your bodyweight into it to make it turn. These shopping carts are those shopping carts, thirty years later. We were lucky that we had one wheel that still swiveled.

As we were pushing these carts from the airplane to the taxi through the sea of hungry humanity; the sense of *mission* increased. The mission was to get the boxes to the taxi and to get the contents of the boxes- food, medication, and clothing- to the orphans and the students in need.

When we finally got the cargo in the truck and piled the ten of us on top of the boxes and headed off; we saw that on every different corner throughout Port-au-Prince were the U.S. Army, the British Army, or the Canadian Army with AK-47s keeping the peace because the chaos was so great following the tragedy. We discovered that in the absence of food and clean water, chaos was inevitable.

When that first work day was finally finished, and we had the opportunity to relax in the folding chairs back at the compound where we stayed, each of us called home to the states and said the same thing. We told our wives and families *"Everything is fine, do not be concerned about us. It is safe here, there is nothing to worry about."* None of us were going to talk about the Armies and their AK47s, until we were back home safely.

As the days went on and the urgent needs were being met at the mission, we started to strike a rhythm with our labor. We utilized the limited resources we had, instead of complaining about the resources we did not have. Our efforts were becoming more practical and efficient. We were learning to be more resourceful in using the outdated building materials we had available. In essence, we were becoming more creative out of necessity.

After the third day of labor intensive, creative building in Haiti, at our rest period at night, the ten of us common men reflected on the incredible impact we have made in such a short time for the school and orphanage, using what little we had. We also discussed and concluded 'why' we did what we did.

It was unanimous, we all agreed, we served because there was a need, and God called us to be practical and resourceful to the best of our abilities. There was no deep prior theological discussions before this particular mission trip, no fanfare send off, there was no praise for us 'brave' men who went to help after the horrible tragedy. The motivation was really quite simple. There was a need, we were capable, and *love* moved us from our comfort zones.

I spoke of love much of the time from the safety of my comfortable American Church surroundings. But now, I was coming to grips with my own hypocrisy. I wrote this devotion on that third night in Haiti, in our reflection time. It is loosely based on the question Jesus asked Peter three times on the beach in the last chapter of the book of John. And it also reminds me of something I read years ago in a book, *Christian Meditation*, by James Finley. It scribbled off my pen like this:

- Jesus said "come"-We came with great excitement.

- Jesus said "if you love me, feed my sheep". We respond "of course we love you lord, but first we must organize."

- Jesus said "if you love me, feed my sheep". We respond "of course we love you lord, but first we must keep organized to keep order".

- Jesus said "if you love me, feed my sheep". We respond "of course we love you lord, but first we must build houses in your honor so we can organize, so we can keep order in the house that we built for you."

- Jesus said "if you love me, feed my sheep". We respond "in order to keep order, organize your house, we must keep out those who do not understand our order".

- Jesus said "if you love me, feed my sheep"...we could not hear His voice, there was too much chatter.

- Today, my friends and I heard the voice of Jesus. It was in the hope of the people of Haiti. Today, we heard songs of praise behind the rubble. Today we heard His simple call, and we simply responded. And, we became _alive_ in the process.

Howard Thurman once said "don't ask what the world needs. Ask what makes you come alive, and go do it. Because what the world needs are people who have come alive."

I love what Marianne Williamson wrote as a reflection on *A Course in Miracles,* and later, Nelson Mandela made famous. She wrote:

"Our deepest fear is not that we are inadequate. Our deepest fear is that we are powerful beyond measure. It is our light, not our darkness, that most frightens us. We ask ourselves, who am I to be brilliant, gorgeous, talented, and fabulous? Actually, who are you not to be? You are a child of God. Your playing small doesn't serve the world. There's nothing enlightened about shrinking so that other people won't feel insecure around you. We are all meant to shine, as children do. We are born to make manifest the glory of God that is within us. It's not just in some of us, it's in everyone. And as we let our own light shine, we unconsciously give other people

permission to do the same. As we are liberated from our own fear, our presence automatically liberates others."[xiii]

When we respond to God's call simply by rising to the human needs that are placed before us, we are performing the deepest type of worship; we are practicing loving our neighbor. We are becoming alive, telling our own unique story, which is a reflection of God's eternal love story.

I assure you that no one on their deathbed leaves saying "I wish I would have accumulated more! I wish I would have been more selfish in my days! I wish I would have loved less!"

Everyone who reflects on their life in the end, focuses on what made them *come alive.* In almost all cases, it was about the heart-felt, meaningful work, not necessarily the work that supplied their paycheck. And the most passionate focus of reflection at the end of life is giving thanks for the loved ones in the dying person's life. In the end, money means almost nothing in most of the cases.

Ultimately, the dying person's life was expressed most richly in the people who shared their life. In essence, their story was meaningful when they experienced love from others, and were able to demonstrate that love back outwards with purposeful labor that produced real and meaningful fruits from their labor. Their life mattered. The world is better, loved ones are better off, because the person saying goodbye, became *alive* while he was living.

When it is your turn to die, it would be so sad to think that your final testimony one gives about you at your memorial service, would be about something other than what was genuinely you! The thing that made you come alive.

No regrets. I pray none of us waste time on merry-go-rounds, that will only take us back to the same spot over and over without the thrill of mountains to climb and valleys to plummet. I would think the roller coaster is a better metaphor for *becoming alive*. There is more risk, thrill, exhilaration, and energy, and a greater chance of purpose, satisfaction and meaning, once it is time to exit the ride.

Go fix things with primitive tools! Get creative out of necessity in order to serve others. There is truly greatness, for those who risk *coming alive* for the benefit of their neighbor.

Rich Man and Lazarus

Jesus tells a story about a simple poor man named *Lazarus*. [iv]

Lazarus died, went to heaven, and was with Abraham. Meanwhile, a rich man, who ignored the poor man on earth, died and went to hell, simply because he never showed mercy to the poor while he was on earth.

Lazarus was with *Abraham* in heaven. The rich man asked Abraham, from hell, to warn his brothers of the price they will pay for ignoring the poor, but Abraham said *"your brothers have Moses and the prophets."* In essence, Abraham was saying *"if your brothers are good Jews, they will know to feed the poor, cloth the naked, take care of the widows, the sick and the old because all of Jewish scriptures and prophets tell us that caring for others is our Jewish duty!"*

Abraham is the father of the Jewish people. He is also the patriarch of the Christian and Muslim faiths, as well. All three religions share our roots with Abraham. We all have in common Father Abraham.

This Lazarus story tells the first century follower that Jesus' message of *caring for the poor* is the same message that God's prophets in the Old Testament, would preach. This Lazarus story is a loud shout for social justice through mercy. It is a unified message for Christians and Jews alike, it says: at the heart of God is a desire for us to be merciful and compassionate for the less fortunate. It is impossible to understand the heart of God, without knowing his quest for mercy.

Pastor and author, Jim Wallis, tells the story of when he was in seminary. He challenged the students to find all the scripture that has to do with Social Justice. There are 2000 verses in the whole Bible regarding feeding the poor, clothing the naked, standing for the poor, caring for the sick. The seminary students decided to take an old Bible and cut out everything in the book-from Genesis to Revelation- that had to do with social justice or acts of mercy for those in need.

This now famous Bible was held up in sermons; held up for people to see, to decide how deep this message of mercy runs. The Bible was just held together with loose paper shreds.

We miss the bulk of the religious message when we overly concern ourselves with our *own* story and miss the cries of the Lazarus's in our lives.

At the Village, a few days after the death of our 104 year old, Astrid, residents were demonstrating mercy. As explained before, the loss of Astrid brought sadness, especially to her best friend Fran, who was 100 at the time. How her heart was hurting after sitting with someone for three years in the sun under the breezeway, in their favorite chairs, and suddenly Astrid's chair was empty. After her death, there seemed to be clouds that formed, blocking the sunshine. After a few days of shadows, we started to see the sunshine through the clouds again. It was proof that the sun was always shining, we just see darkness sometimes, depending on where we stand.

The days after Astrid took her last breath, a few ladies already set a routine to sit with Fran after lunch. Usually between three and four in the afternoon. They sat and told their favorite stories about Astrid and the smiles returned. It was compassion that motivated, and it was returned tenfold, through the fulfillment one gets through meaningful service.

Around the same time of the loss of Astrid, we had a challenge of having both elevators down for a few days. It was the first and only time this happened. But, it was the mercy of the employees that allowed God's love to be demonstrated in a very practical and direct way for our six floors of neighbors.

Residents still had doctor appointments. People still had to eat. Life had to go on. And a large portion of our people were not capable of using the stairs.

We watched as men, blue collar and white collar workers, put down their pens, loosened their ties, and carried residents down six floors in the stairwells in wheelchairs, bringing neighbors safely down to the first floor to go to their doctor appointments and other errands that could not wait.

We witnessed as the kitchen and dining room staff ran meals up the six flights of steps a few hundred times to the people who could not come down for dinner.

We watched as a community of workers, long after their shift change, stayed to make sure resident's dogs were walked. Employees could have easily said "sorry, not my job." Instead, you saw, not only the staff go beyond the call of duty, but all of our visitors and resident's capable family members work tirelessly as well. Even our mail lady, Linda, called her teenage son to call his teenage friends to come out and volunteer to help deliver mail, walk dogs, and carry meals up and down all the floors.

The good news is that the elevators were fixed and all was back to normal. But the endearing inspirational picture was one of the *Village community* reaching down deep, showing mercy. We witnessed able bodied employees and volunteers pulling together to care for the part of the community that was no longer capable of fully caring for themselves. For three days, the community functioned as the merciful servant for all of those in need.

Paul of the New Testament called the believing community that practiced goodwill for all, the *Body of Christ*. In those few days, each member served a function that complemented the other. The common good was shared by all.

According to the story of the rich man and Lazarus that Jesus told, taking care of the Lazarus's in our world, is not just an act of charity, it is not just an act of compassion, showing mercy is an encounter with the living God. Mercy was quite literally the difference between heaven and hell.

When one is in need, and someone who is fully capable in providing relief takes the time to provide assistance, the very *act of assistance* becomes it own reward. And, we don't simply show mercy because it is the right thing to do; by showing mercy, our very lives are exponentially more meaningful.

Demonstrating an act of compassion is the answer to the *blandness* of life. Being helpful, adds the flavor.

The blandness is so prevalent for so many of us, especially in America, where we lack so little in comparison to other neighbors of other nations. We run to find *meaning* in outside *stuff*. We chase rabbit trails of self indulgence to find happiness, only to wake up the next morning to discover that our self-indulgence took us further and further away from true meaning.

Religion is not just about sitting around, knowing you are assured of heaven by God's grace because you are faithful; the full experience of faith is taking that grace and giving it legs into a world that needs it. For the Christian, it is being Christ's hands and feet. For the follower of Judaism, it is following the teachings of the prophets and doing *Mitzvot* (good deeds, like taking care of the poor and the elderly, visiting the sick, and giving to charity).

In all religions, God's plan for mercy for those in need, are carried out by the followers. The love that empowers us to perform acts of kindness, becomes its own reward.

Viktor Frankl, a Jewish Psychiatrist who survived the Holocaust and went onto write over 30 works that gave us deep and profound insights into mental health, claimed a revelation transfixed him as he was marching in the Nazi Concentration Camp in the snow without shoes in his third year of imprisonment under the most oppressive regime man has ever known. He wrote:

"For the first time in my life I saw the truth as it is set into song by so many poets, proclaimed as the final wisdom by so many thinkers. The Truth is that love is the ultimate and the highest goal which man can aspire. The salvation of man is in love and through love."

I ask you, if we listen to the words of Viktor Frankl's, are not his words a reflection of the collective message of the Old Testament Prophets? Are his words not the cornerstone of Jesus' ministry of loving God and neighbor? Or, possibly the description of the third of the Five Pillars of Islam, which is *Alms* giving? Does Viktor Frankl's words resonate with the compassionate teachings of Buddha in the Dharma, which is *Do No Harm?* Does Dr. Frankl's words reflect the root of Hindu culture of *truth seeking*? Or maybe the wisdom of Taoism?

Love, through its tapestry of many expressions, is what holds us together as a global community. Mercy unites.

The healthiest part of all inter-religious dialogue is to discover the fact that *love* stands in the center of all of their sacred scripture and practices.

The Dali Lama said "my religion is simple: kindness." When Mother Teresa was wiping the secretions from a dying Hindu child's nose in Calcutta, a newspaper reporter who was almost ready to vomit said "I would not do what you are doing for a million dollars. And Mother Teresa responded simply and profoundly "neither would I".

Jesus shares that weighty story of Lazarus in Luke's gospel. It is about hell. But, when we take this story as Jesus shares it, we see hell is reserved for the one who simply does *not* show *mercy*.

That is it. The rich man had no love in his heart, for the neighbor in need. According to Jesus and Abraham in this story of Lazarus, 'hell' is the absence of love. In essence, complete isolation from love, is isolation from God, and His people. This is hell.

"Whoever does not love does not know God, for God is love"- so says John the disciple (I John 4:8). *Hell* is not knowing God, not knowing love. According to John, *Hell* and all its ugliness and fears, flees from the face of love, who is God. *"Fear drives us away from God's love. God is love...whoever lives in love lives in God, and God in them. There is no fear in love but perfect love, drives out fear"* (I John 4:16-18).

When we know this, it is hard to believe in a message spit at you with *hell fire and brimstone* from a preacher who seems to handle the love of God as a weapon of control; as if God's love was painful.

Maybe we need to listen to those illustrating the good news with a smile and a tear, as they tell the story of God's amazing grace. Those are the people we can believe.

Maybe we need to roll up our sleeves, loosen our ties, and help carry wheelchairs up and down stairs with common folks who simply serve, because love said so. Those are the *preachers* who understand God's deeply moving mercy.

Good Verses Ego

What is your reaction when you are overlooked for a job promotion that you feel you deserve? How do you feel when betrayed by someone you thought was a friend? What happens when a group has a difference of political or religious views of your own and they insist on you seeing things their way? Does your body feel a certain surge of adrenaline or anxiety? Can you hear your voice changing, maybe louder, maybe more assertive? If you feel hurt or betrayed, do you feel the need to justify, defend, or return a counter attack? What is your inner voice saying in the face of conflict?

Whatever it is you feel deep inside of you, it feels threatened, and wants to be justified, even at the point of sacrificing your bodies health, wellbeing, and blood pressure. To be right or *justified* becomes more important than being at peace.

Then, what do we do with conflict? Do we fight or rollover and play dead? Or, maybe there is a third way. We could *act* by not *reacting* at all. A *way* in which we do not fight, nor rollover, but instead, we stand firm in love.

All the great spiritual teachers lived this inner peace, in moments of conflict. When we stand firm in love, we see each other in ways that we cannot see if we have our bruised *egos* do our bidding for us.

That surge of adrenaline, that 'fight or flight', never has to surface in the face of conflict, really. We do not need to go blind with anger.

One of my physical therapy patients that I used to visit a few years back **at the Village** had a beautiful story of transitioning from a life of *aggression and hostility*, to a life of *peace and meaning*.

Margaret was 81 years old when I saw her. She just had a total knee replacement, and I was scheduled to see her three days a week for six weeks, as her physical therapist.

After a couple of visits, as we became more comfortable with each other, she invited me to look at her bookshelf. On her bookshelf, were many-many spiral notebooks and journals of all sorts. She shared with me that she had started journaling at age 37. She claimed there was better than one full notebook a year since she started. She was on her 51st notebook.

She started journaling just two years after her divorce. She was bitter and angry at the whole world, hostile to people, feuding with family. In the early notebooks, the print was bold, aggressive, and the language was harsh.

Forty-six years later, she told me that the most impressive thing that she witnessed about herself is the fact that she is no longer the angry person she was back then. That had passed, and now she is very content and peaceful.

She had to thank the love of others in her faith community, her village. She was being led by a 'gentle spirit', as she put it. Over time, it was the gathered people, who were unwavering in their patience with her troubled spirit. In time, her writing softened. The language lost its venom. You could physically see, the darker writing, the aggressive sharp-angled penmanship, give way to softer, more rounded lettering. Even some hearts dotted the *'I's* and as the years increased, she added some soft scripture verses that illustrated a deeper expression of her feelings. Her bruised ego, her troubled spirit, slowly slipped away, and a pleasant spirit emerged.

Egos divide us. Egos make us into enemies. With forgiveness and a gentle spirit, enemies become neighbors. Instead of 'us and them' we become *one* gathered people, a village. It is only then, that we can establish a true community, a *Thin Place*. Once we have tasted this fellowship, we find it easier to work towards unity instead of finding reasons to be offended by each other's differences. In a *Thin Place*, we are not afraid to speak honestly out of love.

When we do not have egos to feed, we can speak honestly out of human weakness. When we trust in God's love to move us, there is no more room for us to inflict harm on others. We learn to feed eachother.

At the Village, about a month after the temporarily down elevators led the community to pull together, I witnessed a scene that is a subtle example of this fellowship of which I speak; a fellowship that has no *ego* boundaries.

Clara is a regular attendant of the chapel service, where most members of the village gather each week. She is in her mid-nineties and always sits in the front row. One Sunday, she started to cough, while I was in the middle of delivering the message of the day.

She continued to cough.

While I was getting towards the end of my sermon, Maxwell, who was seven years old at the time, walked from the back of the church and made his way slowly down the outside row of chairs, and down to the very front row, carrying a cup of cold water for his friend Clara. She showed great appreciation for the water that helped stop her cough.

I stopped what I was saying, because by this time, I could see that all eyes were on Maxwell and Clara, and the cup of water.

After a long pause, I simply said, "there is your sermon right there, friends. You will not remember a word I said today, but you just experienced the peaceful message of God's love that I was trying to express in words. A seven year old boy helping a friend, who is almost ninety years older than him, said it better without words."

You see, this world of peace that we speak of, is the world in which *we* are never *defined* as separate from our neighbors.

There is nothing *sensational* about helping a neighbor. When we think about a seven year old boy bringing a cup of water to a near hundred year old woman, it restores a little bit of hope in humanity that we had lost while watching the violent morning news. Peace comes when we can get behind and believe in the goodwill of people again.

Indeed, *revolutions* of goodwill start in small ways by a small group. In fact, that is the only way they had ever started. *"We all cannot do great things, but we can all do little things with great love."* Mother Teresa said that.

Like the water cup, small random acts of kindness snowball to a greater awareness of higher consciousness, or greater awareness of God's love in the world.

Later that same Sunday, I received a random text message, while I was thinking of Maxwell and the cup of water. The text was from a number I did not recognize. It simply said 'hey'.

After looking at it, I texted back, "Hey, who is this?" After a few seconds, another text came back and it said, "It is Eric, who is this?"

I sent a text back "It is Tom, I think you might have texted the wrong number."

A text came back "oh, sorry, my mistake."

For fun I texted him back "No problem Eric, have a *blessed* day!"

After a few seconds, another text came back from Eric the stranger that said "God bless you too, Tom, you have a blessed day!"

Now I am sure that meant almost nothing to him, but now *you* know about it and he might have told some people about the stranger's text message and we all restored a little bit more hope in humanity through the simplest, silliest things.

Theoretically, Maxwell's getting water for Claire, could have started a chain reaction of goodwill, that could rivaled all the collective *evil-will* that was manifested that same day.

Can this be true?

In theory, it is true. In order for evil or hate to compound, the recipient of a thoughtless act, has to *feel* offended and then acted upon it. Thus, starting the chain reaction of thoughtless encounters around the globe. An ego must be bruised, in order to pass on the damage.

Likewise, a random act of *kindness* is compounded when the recipient of the thought*ful* act, had felt loved and then acted upon it. Thus, starting the chain reaction of thoughtful encounters around the globe.

You see, the *ego* is nothing more than a protective, *false* self. The ego is something we must learn to dissolve, so we can go about opening our hearts and the hearts of others.

The ego separates, love unites.

The ego must be absent, in order to pass on the goodwill. In conflict, can you feel that something deep inside you is also in conflict? That is the ego. It feels threatened and wants to be justified, even at the point of sacrificing your body's health and wellbeing. It causes a rise in blood pressure, risk of heart attack and stroke, and creates possible gastrointestinal problems. To be *right* or *justified* becomes more important than being at peace. The ego is truly a parasite to its host, which is your body, mind, and spirit.

When we can recognize that carrying hurt is a personal choice, we are free to set it down. We cast that burden to God. We can plainly see that insults, bitterness, and opinions are always available to lug around, if we feel the need to pick them up.

Eventually, anxiety can cause a person to mentally, and physically ulcerate and weaken. We have the freedom to leave this hostile baggage alone and choose the way of peace. This is the only way to permanent wellness.

This *way of peace*, takes an inner discipline that is far greater than the discipline aggression requires.

We were created to live healthy, in unity with those around us. In community, a random act of kindness is compounded quickly, because of close proximity. Thus, starting the chain reaction of thought*ful* encounters throughout the entire village and beyond. In a community of kindness, everyone nourishes everyone, through our basic variables for health: *healthy shared food, meaningful exercise, and yes-love.* We learn to warm in each other's glow.

There is a good story about this, told by many different story-tellers. This is how I heard it:

A member of a certain church, who previously had been attending services regularly, stopped going. After a few weeks, the minister decided to visit him.

It was a chilly evening. The preacher found the man at home alone, sitting before a blazing fire. After guessing the reason for his preacher's visit, the host led him to one of the two chairs facing the fireplace. They both sat, staring into the fire.

The preacher said nothing. In the grave silence, they both watched the dance of the flames around the burning logs.

After some time, the preacher took the fire tongs, carefully picked up a brightly burning ember, and placed it alone on one side of the hearth. Then he sat back in his chair, still silent. The host watched all this in quiet contemplation. As the one lone ember's flame flickered and diminished, there was a momentary glow and then its fire was no more. Soon it was cold and dead.

Not a word had been spoken since the initial awkward greeting. The preacher glanced at his watch and realized it was time to leave. He picked up the cold, dead ember with the fire tongs and placed it back in the middle of the fire. Immediately it began to glow, once more with the light and warmth of the burning coals around it.

As the preacher shifted to begin to leave, his host said with a tear running down his cheek *"Thank you so much for your visit and especially for the fiery sermon. I will be back in church next Sunday."*[N]

The man, who isolated himself, realized that gathering for worship and fellowship with his congregation, was something much deeper than hymns, words, coffee and cookies. His weekly gathering was a chance for him to warm-up in the glow of others. It was a chance that allowed him to love and be loved by others who were simply trying to get warm. Sometimes the best sermons are the ones unspoken.

To *experience* God's love, one needs to simply allow himself to warm-up in the glow of others. God's love is expressed through His people, who's heart's glow. The glow is sustained from the goodwill of the community.

God's love for us is an unconditional gift. And when we freely accept His free gift, we are filled with the spirit of hope, and we glow. And, with that glow, we are free to rid ourselves of the *ego*. We can stand firm in love, without condition, judgments, hurts, or anxiety. We learn the way of peace.

Hatred is never appeased by hatred. Hatred is only appeased by love. This is an eternal law of the Buddhists.

Peace be with you, was the first words that Jesus said to his community of disciples, on the first day of Easter. The world at the time of the first century did not change, it was still difficult, cold, and cruel. But now, the disciples hearts were very different. They believed in a peace, beyond the chaos. They saw the dawn of redeeming grace. They glowed.

Peace is a *knowing* that everything will be alright, regardless of the outside circumstances. *Peace be with you.*

Do You Love Me?

Personal peace starts with a *deeper* understanding of every conflicted situation. For when we go deeper, we see that all persons in conflict are after the same thing, and that is...*to be understood*. We all share this desire.

A little three year old girl, who did not speak English, was entering the day care for the first time. She held tightly to her daddy and then was passed on to the day care worker. As the dad left, the little girl kicked and screamed as she went into the day care. For the first day, the minute her feet hit the floor of the daycare carpet, she could not be calmed down. She constantly was working to try to get her shoes off her feet, and the staff constantly insisted that she keep them on because all the other kids kept their shoes on. So they struggled with her for the entire second day to keep her shoes on, all the while she was screaming and fighting to remove her shoes. The only time she was not crying, is when she finally got her down for a nap; but the crying would start again as soon as she woke to find her shoes were on her feet.

The daycare staff called a conference with the parents. It was only the mother who could make the meeting. As the front door opened, in walked the mother, a small women, who was wearing a beautiful Kimono (a traditional Japanese dress) and as she got to the door, she stepped out of her shoes, as is the Japanese tradition, as she entered the a dwelling.[vi]

The perceptions of the workers at the daycare were that the little girl was simply being difficult, where the reality is that she just wanted to honor her mother's teachings by removing her shoes as she entered the building. The workers were extremely grateful for this truth that was shown them. They were grateful that they went deeper to understand the problem, fully. It was no longer a problem from then on.

Most of us are familiar with the children's book *The Giving Tree* by Shel Silverstein.[vii] The children's book that starts with a relationship between a child and a tree where they spent time together daily-enjoying eachother-simply being in the presence of one another. Before long the boy discovers he would do well if he had some money, and the tree suggests selling her apples.

So the boy takes her apples.

Then the boy grows up and she offers her branches for lumber. The boy takes her branches. Then the boy discovered that he needs to travel, she offers her trunk to make a boat for him. The boy takes her trunk.

At the end of the boys life, when he was too old to swing in the trees branches, too tired to build, and too exhausted to make money; it was then and only then when he realized that it was the tree that was there for him all along. He chose to rest with her.

Like the old man in the Giving Tree, his perspective as he sits upon the stump of the tree that has given everything of herself over and over to the boy who never recognized her *grace*, her unconditional love. It was only at the end, when he is finished with a life of self-centeredness, did he gain a perspective of her loving nature, God's nature.

After being betrayed by Peter, crucified, and resurrected; Jesus returned to his dear friend, Peter. He simply asked the question *"Peter, do you love me?"* [viii]

One would think after being betrayed by Peter, Jesus would have been justified in saying something like *'now look Peter! I want to see a little gratitude. Do you have any idea what I had been through?'* But this was not the message we learn from Jesus. We simply hear the question *"Peter, do you love me?"*

It was the same question *Tevye* asked his wife *Goldie* in the play *Fiddler on the Roof*, "Do you love me?" And Goldie rattled off those things she did in service to her husband for twenty-five years.

"I washed your clothes, I cooked your meals, I cleaned your house, I milked your cow" she lamented.

All those things were true and good reminders of her *devotion* to him, but Tevye persisted, with his simple question "Do you love me?"

And, eventually, Goldie answered "yes".

We have but one question to answer. Our faith does not hinge on whether we attend the right place of worship, or give the right amount, or whether we served on committees at church or synagogue, or attended mission trips; our one question we need to answer, is God's question to us, which is *"Do you love me?"*

When we fully understand the limitless Grace that God bestows on each of us; when we fully understand that our Creator, did not *have* to create, he *chose* to; it is at that point when we can start to sincerely answer the question with an emphatic yes! We can say, yes, we feel love for the Creator God, who had provided for us, all our days. If not true, life would not be.

Like in *The Giving Tree*, when we love God, we take time to swing from His branches, we take time to be grateful for the life and the provisions we have been given. When we recognize the deep love the Creator has for us, we love back, gratefully.

Kent Keith wrote The *Paradoxical Commandments* in the sixties, and was later adopted by Mother Teresa. He said:

"People are illogical, unreasonable, and self-centered...Love them anyway. The good you do today will be forgotten tomorrow...Do good anyway. What you spend years building may be destroyed overnight...Build anyway."[ix]

We have a deeper understanding than the chaos and the noise that is made in the *shallow* end of the pool of life. In the shallow end, all the splashing takes place. This is where the drama of prejudice, pride, envy, lust, ego, greed, and injustice exists. God calls us away from the shallow end and into the deeper waters. On this side, we start understanding His grace.

Still waters run deep. In deep waters, we learn to live in a world of gratitude and thanksgiving, seeing God's goodness through the storms of life, as well as experiencing the beauty of God's people as we gather in community. We experience gratitude, regardless of the outside circumstances.

Once we experience the freedom that gratitude gives us in life, we can start painting over the ugly cracks and stains that bitterness may have caused. We can live this beautiful prospective every day. We can be grateful in knowing we are cared for in our meaningful lives by our generously *giving* Creator.

The Prodigal Son

I recently visited a large evangelical church. This church had a well meaning youth pastor who was giving a message to a room full of troubled teens. His message was the story of the *Prodigal Son.* Those who know this story that Jesus shares, know that it is a story about a father who always has his arms open for his children, even a wayward self-indulgent, narcissistic, *prodigal son.* [x]

This young preacher at this large church, preached about the amazing Prodigal Son story. Unfortunately, instead of focusing on the main point Jesus was making in the parable - about the father's unconditional love, the young preacher spent nearly an hour talking about the *sin* of the son, without ever reaching the unconditional *love* of the Father. He never spoke of God's grace.

His hour was spent on the prodigal son, who ended up in the *pigpen* after squandering his father's money away on self-indulgent behaviors. This young preacher spoke of how all of us are sliding around in our own pig slop and it is up to us to climb out or be *left behind*.

His point was that God does not approve of our pigpen lifestyles. God hates our pigpen behaviors we choose to live. In other words 'Get right, or get left behind.'

The preacher was right, God is not happy with our pigpen behaviors, our sinful nature. He gives us provisions and free choice and we manage to over-indulge ourselves with His abundance. But, the story of the Prodigal Son is not about that. It has a much deeper, more promising message.

I can only imagine the troubled teenagers who left that day. They left with a double load of pain and guilt. Knowing that they are living in a pigpen, and also, that God requires them to get out of their problems *before* they are accepted by God.

These teens, who have been longing for deep spiritual food, had only received a lecture on the God of judgment. They learned that God leaves us dry, if we do not pick *ourselves* out of the pigpen!

I wanted desperately to go to the young preacher and share with him of the deeper meaning of one of the most incredible *parental love* stories ever told. The Prodigal Son is a story about the Father's lavish grace! It is about a God who loves us, unconditionally! A father who throws a party for us, once we turn back towards home, knowing we cannot do 'life' alone.

I wanted this young preacher to *feel* the freedom in that story that Jesus was telling, so he could pass it on to the teenagers he was preaching to. This is the only way we receive the peace that passes all understanding.

I think if those troubled teens heard the rest of that story, they could start to see themselves with real value, as their Creator does. And then they would reach out to be *lifted* from their pigpens, by God's loving hands. They would not need to continue the desperate painful struggle, alone and ashamed.

Spiritually injured people, who enter the doors of a church, synagogue, or temple for the first time, enter because they have been unable to climb from their pigpens on their own. They are in desperate need of help. And God is *The Father* who welcomes the child with love unconditionally. God is eagerly waiting for them to come home.

This is grace. The more we try to dissect grace, the more it falls apart because of our inability to define it with our limited reasoning and understanding. That is the nature of God's grace. It is beyond words, beyond reason. One needs to only open his ears, hands, and heart and realize that scripture tells us that we have a heavenly father who has an unconditional love for us, the wayward *Prodigal Son*.

I want to tell you about another church that I had the privilege to be a part of one Sunday. This one was in Haiti. We attended the service during the same mission trip, six weeks after the devastating earthquake of on January 12, 2010.

The ten of us American men attended an open air church full of kids from the school that we were helping. At the service, our new Haitian friends prayed for two things: first, they gave thanks that they survived the earthquake, even though many of their families and friends, did not; and secondly, they prayed that their new ten friends from the United States would remain safe and happy while we were in Haiti.

I will say it again, these beautiful children who lived well below the poverty line and had just experienced loss of family and friends from the devastating earthquake, prayed for us! We suddenly realized the self-centered nature of our own prayer life, juxtaposed to the humility of these children and their most sincere prayer they prayed while standing in a world of brokenness. That Sunday, we were experiencing a *Thin Place*; we were standing on Holy Ground.

Many of these children entered the open-air chapel after an hour walk from their homes in the mountains; and the only motivation for such a long walk was to sing songs together, to hear a message of hope, to stand with their new American friends, and maybe get a piece of bread with peanut butter on it. We were humbled.

This preacher in Haiti, preached the story of hope, even though hope appeared lost for these Haitian children. They heard the same message of the *Prodigal Son*, just like the large church in America, but the difference was the *lavish grace* of the father was the message. These children discovered beyond a shadow of a doubt, that they are not forgotten, and that their father in heaven loves them.

At that service, the beautiful children of Haiti taught us to sing a song of praise and worship that we sang in the states called *'Here I am to Worship.'*[xi] As we did our best to sing the words scribbled on a chalkboard in Creole, their native tongue, I watched as these precious children, sang with their eyes closed and arms uplifted *"here I am to worship, here I am to bow down, here I am to say that you're my God"*. They sang with such an intensity and honesty. No matter how far down life can drop them, they know that God is still with them. Not with money, not with security, but with His lavish grace. And His grace is sufficient.

Jim Wallis, author of *God's Politics*, told a story about his father's home church. This church experienced an unfortunate occurrence. A young woman became pregnant out of wedlock with her boyfriend. Both, young people were faithful members of the church. Both of them were extremely sorry for the mistake they had made.

It was decided that the elders would put those two young people up on display and rebuke the terrible wrong they did, making sure there was a clear message to all the other young people that their church has a zero tolerance for this kind of sinful nature.

Jim Wallis' father was an elder in that particular church and was adamantly opposed to do this to this young couple, who were trying their best to do the right thing following their mistake.

Jim's father said "don't you think those kids know already they did wrong? Don't you think they know where we stand? Don't you think they will pay dearly already by having to raise a child at such a young age?"

The other elders pushed back "oh no, we are not backing down, they have sinned and they need to be punished" We will put them on public display so this sin does not happen again by other unmarried young people in the church!"

Jim's father said "all right then, we will do it. But, just to be fair, as we expose and rebuke the sin of these two in their vulnerability, I say we all take the opportunity to stand *with* them on display and admit *our* sins as well as a public confession for the whole church to hear. And just in case you forgot your sins, you know I have been counseling most of you over the years, and I will be happy to remind you of your sins."

The motion was made to not make public rebuking of the teens."[xii]

At another real church - another real community - had a deeper understanding of God's Grace.

Another young woman, pregnant out of wedlock, was a faithful member of a Presbyterian Church in a small rural community. Everyone knew the situation and the pain and financial hardship that this situation caused the young lady. Her boyfriend left, she had no family, just her church, and one unfortunate situation.

The baby was born, and upon the Sunday for baptism, the preacher went about his duties as he always does with the Service Book of Worship with a baptism. He read out loud *"who will stand for this child to assure the commitments and promises made will be carried out?"* Following that line, the sponsors are supposed to answer the question with the answer that is in bold print: ***"I will, and I ask God to help and Guide me."***

The pastor looked up. There was no sponsor. The mother stood alone; no husband, no parents, no sisters or brothers, no Godparents to respond to the question that was written in the service book. No one was there to speak on their behalf, no one to advocate for them. It was just this young mother and a tiny-tiny baby. Alone.

The embarrassment and awkwardness came over both preacher and young mother, but after just a short moment of silence, you could hear from the back of the church, an older woman, with grown kids, stood and said *"I will, and I ask God to help and Guide me"*. Then another, this time a mother and father of three stood up "I will, and I ask God to help and Guide me". Then another. And another. And after a short time, the entire faith community was on their feet, standing for this tiny, forgotten baby and single mother, making good the promise to raise this child as a precious member of the community of faith, teaching him of the ways of God; loving and nurturing him in the faith, letting him and his mother know, that they are both precious in the Father's sight. [xiii]

Truly, that Sunday at that particular church, was a *Thin Place*, where the physical and the spiritual were close at hand, was experienced by all.

Soren Kierkegaard, the Danish Theologian in the 19th Century, described that a trusting faith in God is a lot like a man hanging off a cliff with a roaring fire above him, where he cannot get back to safe ground. And, he hears from below him, a voice that speaks calmly and with authority "let go of the cliff, I got you."

The man hanging off the cliff looks down and sees nothing. Blackness. No light at all. He is scared. He says "I can't let go, I can't see you!" And the voice replies "it's okay, I can see you."

When we trust in God's grace, we change our prospective. We connect with the community we have been given as a gift from God. We see God's fingerprints everywhere. We see our community of faith, filled with humanity's imperfections, but made perfect through God's unconditional love.

Some of the most remedial tasks, can become a devotion to God. Mother Teresa described her calling in Calcutta, India as *an opportunity to care for Jesus in all his many distressing disguises.*

It is not a *task* to care for others, it is an *honor*. This is often the case with our nursing staff at the village, who do the daily work that many would find difficult.

One on the nursing staff, Veda, grew up Hindu. Both Veda and her sister Chandra are deeply compassionate and see their job as a calling from God. Their job would be even more trying each day without the awareness of being called by God to work with the seniors who need their help. God's unconditional love is expressed through their hands to their patients, in a very concrete way.

When Veda was young, she moved to America with her family. The church missionaries were in her town. They talked about this man Jesus, she saw his picture, and was moved to tears by his compassionate stories. She wanted to receive him. She stood in line for the bread and the wine for communion and was abruptly refused because she was from a different religion. It was not until she was older that she learned that the God of Jesus' loves everyone. As she put it, "I learned that Jesus is not just for white people, but Indians as well." Veda takes communion now, with the rest of us.

Often times, hopeful beggars come through our doors of worship for the first time, broken, honest, and desperate for deliverance from the *pigpen* they find themselves. Sometimes, religious leaders can only offer double servings of shame, more pain, more ridicule because the beggar doesn't possess the *orthodox* or proper understanding that the insiders do.

But, if a beggar is fortunate enough to stumble into a community that truly believes in the *lavish grace* of God, then the beggar, like the *Prodigal Son*, can experience God's unconditional love. God's grace is sufficient.

We are all beggars stumbling into places of worship, all in search of *God's lavish grace*.

Inspiration at 100

At the Village, one of our cherished residents, Miriam, went on a long summer trip. Upon her returning, I went up to her apartment on the fifth floor in the late afternoon to hear about her summer adventures.

She was still unpacking her bags from her long flights that morning. She said to me "gosh I am tired. I had to get on my plane, early this morning. I have been up since 5:00 am!"

Then she proceeded to tell me all about the wonderful experiences she had with her family, son David, daughter Lynne, four grandchildren and seven great-grandchildren. She told me of the summer festivities they had together in Chautauqua, New York.

Every year for decades, she has been going to spend the summer in Chautauqua, New York where her daughter lives.

Chautauqua is a unique city in America that preserves a real sense of community, face-to-face education and dialogue through summer lecture programs.

Chautauqua had originally started as being a center for Sunday School teachers who came to become educated during the summer months, and it has carried on the tradition of a lifelong pursuit of education for over 135 years.

This particular summer's adventure was filled with all types of lectures, art exhibits, and concerts. But this summer was extra special. Miriam and her family celebrated her 100th birthday. The town celebrated with her.

Interestingly enough, Miriam was not doing as well physically at ninety-nine years old. Her new doctor, found that she was significantly over-medicated, and went about ridding her of all the unnecessary medications. Afterwards, her health had been greatly improved.

I often sit with my friends at the Village and wonder *what is the fountain of youth that they drink from?* For each centarian (100 year old) we have living with us, there are a dozen or so who are in their 90s and still going strong.

One of the unique traits you quickly notice about most all Centarians is their awareness of their blessings.

So often, you do not hear them talk of pains, sicknesses, and death. Although these things certainly might be on their minds, you hear words of life, love, and continued passions. Their lives are spiritual lives. They are spiritual beings on an earthly journey, and love seems to be the catalyst that keeps them dreaming dreams.

With this understanding, joy and peace come to these spiritual beings as naturally as breathing in and breathing out. One-hundred year olds, typically are inspired. Inspired means *in-spirit*. Many Centarians are literally inspired by God's spirit.

In the words of George Bernard Shaw:

"I want to be thoroughly used up when I die. For the harder I work; the more I love. I rejoice in life for its own sake. Life is no brief candle to me. It is a sort of

splendid torch which I've got a hold of for the moment, and I want to make it burn as brightly as possible before handing it on to future generations."

At the Village, inspiration is easy to spot. Most members of the community, who are inspired, exude a joy that accompanies the grateful feeling they experience by recognizing the simple blessings.

Fran, a year after her 104 year old friend Astrid had passed, shared with me that her favorite things in life, are her Sunday morning service, her friends and family, her table mates that she sits with during her daily dining experiences, and her glass of wine at night.

"I am not an alcoholic, I can quit anytime" she jokingly says. Obviously, at 101 years old, she does not need to quit.

We had a new resident, Barbara, move in the same week that Fran had her 101 birthday. On the day she moved in, she took me by the hand to show me with great excitement her new home. It was her bed, her dresser, her closet, and bathroom. She was beaming. "I am so happy to be here. Everyone is so nice. It feels like home."

Home is much more than the place you lay your head. Home is seen more clearly, not with the eyes, but with the heart. One can be in the finest of houses, with security gates and all the modern conveniences, yet this will still not make it a home. A dwelling becomes a home, when the heart allows it. It is finding a comfort that money cannot buy. A home is a *Thin Place* when we recognize that the physical and the spiritual bunk together. Barbara was excited about her new humble dwelling, because she recognized it as a *Thin Place*. It was home.

Eckhart Tolle asks us to imagine a beggar waiting at the road, begging for the greater part of his forty years of life. As each person passed, the begging began *"spare some change? Could you please spare some money for me, I am hungry."*

One day a stranger came by, and asked him what was in the box he was sitting on? The beggar answered that he did not know, he had been sitting on it for his entire life and had never looked inside. Together they opened the box, and to beggar's surprise, it was filled with gold. The beggar, who had lived in scarcity his entire life, the beggar who had nothing but pain and sorrow, was sitting on abundance his entire life. He just did not have eyes to see.[xiv]

Like the beggar, we too can rejoice. We are also sitting on the box of gold, not in money, but in spirit. Once we have discovered our *home* in God's grace, we have the inner peace that is ours. His grace is sufficient. We need nothing else, just others for us to share our abundance.

A Sense of Belonging

There is a legendary parable of a village in Nigeria. All members of the community are invited to the great feast each year. The great feast is topped off with all the wine you can drink. The wine is poured from a barrel, in which every member of the tribe brings a jug of their best homemade wine to share with the community. Literally, 100 jugs of wine are emptied into a huge barrel. From the barrel wine is poured to each persons glass.

One villager decided that if he were to just simply pour water from his single jug, that one in a hundred jugs will not dilute the overall taste of the wine that terribly much. He reasoned, if he were to do this, he can keep his wine for himself and not have to share. And, he could still drink everyone else's wine.

The time had come to pour. All glasses were filled. The toast was made. The entire village drank at once and, to everyone's surprise, the entire huge barrel was simply water.

All members of the village decided to keep their jug of wine for themselves and add their portion in water.

A village *only* functions when the individual puts the heart of the community before his own.

A wonderful revelation we discover about *community* is that it is found at the root of all religions: Christianity, Judaism, Muslim, Buddhism, Hinduism, etc.

It is in Africa where we get the wonderful Bantu word *Ubuntu* which simply means "to be affirming to others in community." God desires for us to be affirming to one another.

In the book of *Acts* in the Bible, scripture tells us that the new found community of the first Christians ate together, worshipped together, and helped each other sharing common possession, so nobody went without. In other words, a strong sense of community was experienced for the first time, as a new *way* of living.

When *we* learn to trust each other and share in the collective goodwill of all, we experience God's love in community.

Several years ago, while I was in seminary, I served as a volunteer counselor at a 'Hope Hospice' retreat that was put on for kids at camp *Evergreen* in the mountains of Pennsylvania. Twenty-five children who attended the retreat had recently lost a parent, mostly to cancer.

One of the young girls, we will call *Cathy*, was eight year old at the time. She and her sister were both attending the weekend. They had lost their father to Lou Gehrig's Disease when he was thirty-seven. I met the girls at the retreat on the day of my thirty-eighth birthday.

Cathy did not talk much about her father. Her older sister, developed a seizure disorder for no apparent reason. Child Psychologists just knew it had something to do with this loss.

All twenty-five kids were struggling with a feeling of abandonment. Some felt guilt, that somehow, they did something to make God *take* their parent. Loneliness, sadness, grief, despair, anger, guilt, disbelief were all words used describing the harbored feelings of these precious children.

Through the counseling sessions, they all agreed that they are different now, after their losses. Different somehow; not complete, as they were prior to the passing of their parent.

Somewhere during a counseling session on the second day, our group of emotionally broken children began to feel different. It was the honesty of the children and the commitment and love of the counselors, that started to bring a sense of *belonging* into the group. But it wasn't by clever counseling techniques, or that us volunteers had the right things to say. No, the belonging came about in a much more *mystical* way.

When great loss happens, we are left empty. We only start to heal when we encounter, or rediscover, a loving God who suffers *with* us, and not a God who inflicts this pain *upon* us. We discover a love that transcends the hopelessness we are experiencing.

At the retreat, the kids were all drawn to each other out of their tragedies. For the love of the children, we all became a true community of hope, joined by a deep common pain. Yet, deeper still, was a profound spiritual connection to the heart of God. Tears of pain, not yet turned to tears of joy, but certainly, tears cried together. We knew somehow that God was shedding tears with us, as we began our healing.

By the end of the week, we were a true community, witness to God's amazing grace, and faithful to the recovery and healing of each and every member of that group.

God's grace is sufficient. Even in the worst of tragedies, indeed, maybe because of the tragedies, we achieved a sense of belonging.

A Beautiful Spirit

A frail old man went to live with his son, daughter-in-law, and a four-year old grandson. The old man's hands trembled, his eyesight was blurred, and his step faltered. The family ate together nightly at the dinner table. But the grandfather's shaky hands and failing sight made eating rather difficult. Peas rolled off his spoon onto the floor. When he grasped the glass often milk spilled on the tablecloth. The son and daughter-in-law became irritated with the mess. "We must do something about grandfather," said the son. I've had enough of his spilled milk, noisy eating, and food on the floor.

So the husband and wife set a small table in the corner. There, grandfather ate alone while the rest of the family enjoyed dinner at the dinner table. Since grandfather had broken a dish or two, his food was served in a *wooden bowl*.

Sometimes when the family glanced in grandfather's direction, he had a tear in his eye as he ate alone. Still, the only words the couple had for him were sharp admonitions when he dropped a fork or spilled food. The four-year-old grandson watched it all in silence.

One evening before supper, the father noticed his son playing with wood scraps on the floor. He asked the child sweetly, "What are you making?"

Just as sweetly, the boy responded, "Oh, I am making a little bowl for you and mama to eat your food from when I grow up." The four-year-old smiled and went back to work.

The words so struck the parents that they were speechless. Then tears started to stream down their cheeks. Though no word was spoken, both parents knew what must be done.

That evening the husband took grandfather's hand and gently led him back to the family table, never to be disillusioned again.[xv]

As a physical therapist working **at the Village**, I once visited a one-hundred year old self proclaimed *'Christian Mystic'* named Lucy for the first time. We became friends, after that first visit.

Lucy was blind and unable to walk. She was quite talkative and very pleasant to be with, in spite of her mild dementia.

Our first encounter with each other was on her patio, where we proceeded with a physical therapy evaluation.

After a few minutes of conversation and exchanges of personal information, she reached up and put her hand on my head, and said "I want to bless you now."

I thought this was a beautiful thing to offer, so I sat as she put her hand on my head. To my surprise, her hand had a slight *twitch* and a puzzled look came over her face. She smiled a big smile and her glazed-over eyes focused somewhere off in the distance. She then said "I can sense you have a beautiful spirit."

For a couple of minutes I was on a cloud! It is not every day that a one-hundred year old, with what appeared to be psychic abilities, tells you that you had a *beautiful spirit*. I ate it up! I felt wonderfully dignified from our encounter.

As I walked into her apartment from the patio, I saw her son-in-law sitting at the dining room table. I told him exactly what happened with great enthusiasm, like an excited child. His response deflated my delusion.

He said "because of her dementia, she says *'you have a beautiful spirit'* to absolutely everyone".

Sigh...apparently, everyone she encountered and she blessed had the same follow-up statement by her "I can sense you have a beautiful spirit". Maybe I am not so special after all.

On the way to my next appointment, as I contemplated my *ordinariness*, a thought played in my head *'maybe Lucy was right?'*

Maybe she says this to everyone because she *does* sense a *beautiful spirit* in everyone? Maybe she sees the dignity *God* sees in everyone, that we often overlook? Especially the people whose inner-beauty is not so obvious?

Suddenly I felt dignified again. Lucy preached *dignity* to everyone, even from her demented state. God does work in mysterious ways.

A Jewish leader named Simon, invited Jesus to have dinner with him. So Jesus went to his house and reclined at the table.

A sinful woman visited Jesus there. She began to wet his feet with her tears. Then she wiped them with her hair, kissed them, and poured perfume on them. When the Pharisee who had invited him saw this, he said to himself, "If this man were a prophet, he would know who is touching him and what kind of woman she is—that she is a sinner."

Then Jesus told Simon a story about two men who owed money to the bank. One owed the bank 10 times more than the other. Both debts were forgiven.

Jesus asked "which one loved and appreciated more?" Simon replied, "I suppose the one who had the bigger debt canceled." Jesus said "you have judged correctly." [xvi]

We see these three simple stories: the wooden bowl, the 100 year old mystic, and the sinful woman and Jesus, are stories about restoring a sense of dignity to a person who was shown compassion, who was blessed, and who was forgiven.

Dignity is not dispensed based on abilities, merits, or talents; dignity is given freely, because the giver recognizes that every living person is created in God's image, *regardless* of abilities, merits, or talents. Therefore, everyone is worthy of feeling dignified.

The one who was invited back to the family table, regardless of how large a mess he might have made while he ate, had his dignity restored.

The one who is blessed by another, receives the gift of dignity. He senses he has a beautiful spirit.

Like the sinful woman at Jesus' feet, the one who had just turned from shame and guilt, to the light of God's love and forgiveness, has her dignity restored.

God restores dignity to the messy outcast, the impressionable seeker, and the thankful sinner.

Charles Spurgeon once said that when a jeweler shows his best diamonds, he sets them against a black velvet backdrop. The contrast of the jewels against the dark velvet brings out the luster. In the same way, God does his most stunning work where things seem hopeless.

This is how God's love works. The bright luster of compassion, undeserved blessings, and forgiveness contrast against the dark velvet backdrop of shame, guilt, and low self-esteem. With this sharp contrast, God's love can be seen clearly. The giver of dignity, senses a *beautiful spirit* in the other, regardless of the one's abilities, merits, or talents.

Once an entire village recognizes the *beautiful spirits* of each and every member; the community becomes a *Thin Place*, where the physical and the spiritual are close at hand.

Three Principles for a Healthy 100

The Principle of Real Food

In most all religions, light is so often referred to as the source in which the religion is built. Buddhists are en*light*ened, whereas Jesus is the *light* of the world.

Light from the sun warms us and surrounds us. The light illuminates us. We are part of what it illuminates. We are part of the light.

All life is made possible under the sun. We are part of the circle of life that the sun creates. The grasses grow from the sun's rays, the herbivores eat the grass, the carnivore eats the herbivore. The omnivore *(which is what we are)* eats a combination of both herbivores and carnivores, as well as all the other vegetables, fruits, etc. All of life is made possible, thanks to the sun.

Rain also is God's promise of sustaining life. Like the sun, which belongs to none of us, it is shared freely by all of us. Without the rain, life would cease.

When we see rain and sun as gifts, we sense a spiritual renewal and thank the Creator for our provisions in the process.

A while ago, I was waiting at my youngest daughter's soccer practice with all the other moms and dads. This particular Thursday evening, I was reading a book while sitting on the folding lawn chair I kept in my trunk for this very reason.

At the practice, there were three boys who were playing while their older sister practiced. The two older brothers were about 8 and 10 years old, and the littlest sibling could not have been more than five years old.

It was the older brothers who had sticks, and they were whacking at the lower branches of the trees that surrounded the soccer field. Down the line they went, trying hard to knock off as much of the lower branches as they could. Sometimes they were successful in knocking off limbs, sometimes they only were able to knock off a few leaves from the sturdy trees.

As the older boys were working down the line of trees with their path of destruction, it was the little brother who was a tree or two behind them. He was following his older brothers, but not too close. He kept a fair distance between himself and them. Without his older brothers' awareness, he was picking up the newly injured twigs and branches, some with only one or two leaves on them.

Carefully, the younger brother replanted each branch in the ground by the mother tree from which the branch fell. Then he would disappear for a minute or two, and would come back with a full Pepsi cup of water from a hose at the side of a nearby house. He would make sure the branch was carefully standing straight up. Then he would gently pack the soil around the tiny branch. After this, he would slowly pour the water around the planted twig, thoroughly soaking the area all around the little branch.

For better than half of the ninety minute practice, I watched as the five year old boy carefully plant the branches into the ground, and tirelessly go back to the hose to fill his Pepsi cup to come and pour the water over each planted branch. Even after the older brothers lost interest in torturing the tree limbs, the five year old continued to work diligently until, as far as I could see, all the branches were neatly planted next to the mother tree from which they came, and carefully watered.

This little boy's integrity and hope for the life of the little branches that he rescued, reminded me of the hope in God's love, regardless of the destruction that goes on around us. We, who trust in the hope of God's unending love, are not terribly bothered with the destruction that walks just ahead of us. We might think 'what a shame', but we plant the tree anyway. For tomorrow is a new day.

"People are illogical, unreasonable, and self-centered...Love them anyway. The good you do today will be forgotten tomorrow...Do good anyway. What you spend years building may be destroyed overnight...Build anyway."

I did not have the heart to tell that boy, that there is no possible way a tree will grow without the root system that a seed provides. I even contemplated going to him and giving him a quick lesson in Botany, so he could save his energy, but I didn't. I sensed this kindergartener was in fact planting something more important than three dozen branches. He was planting *hope* in the hearts of all the parents and the kids who saw him hard at work, banking on fruit producing in the future, for his caring efforts today.

And now, you read about his story. I think you might tell someone else about this boys endeavor of hope and integrity, and it just might plant a seed of hope in the person you tell.

We continue to experience what happens when love is the motive for our actions. It becomes contagious. The little boy's integrity could not be denied. He had but one purpose, to save the lives of little trees.

There was a story told of an aging company president who decided that he was getting older and needed to start to look for a successor. He had the idea to find a replacement by putting out a contest for all the vice presidents in the company.

He called them all to the board room. As he began the speech, he laid out the future.

"Fellow members of our great company, today I propose a test for you in order to find the next president of the company." He continued "the next president will be the one who can produce the most fruit from one of these lemon tree seeds."

At this point, the aging president took from his pocket 12 seeds and distributed them - one to each of the 12 vice presidents. The aging president continued "You have one year. The one who produces the greatest outcome with a single seed will be the next president of this great company." They all went home excited about the future, all ready to tackle the task they have ahead of them.

Months had gone by. There was much talk around the boardroom, all the vice presidents affirmed their own efforts and stroked their own egos by bragging about how sensational there projects are going; how tall their lemon trees are growing.

Some talked of amazing seedlings that are showing promise needing to be stepped up to a bigger pot.

All went on and on about the amazing gardeners they have become. All, that is, except Frank. Frank had nothing to brag about, for his seed had never blossomed. In fact, it never even started to grow at all. All he had was a pot with soil and a seed that never opened.

The year was almost up, still nothing. Frank had nothing to show, yet all his coworkers told of their amazing prosperity as stewards of their seeds.

The year anniversary had come; the meeting was to take place. Frank decided not to go, but his wife said to him "you go into that meeting today and you let everyone know that you tried but the seed did not grow". He went obediently, with his empty pot of dirt, with his head hung low.

That morning, it looked like a jungle as all the vice presidents sat around the boardroom table with their towering lemon trees sitting in front of them on the conference table, some almost four foot in height. All of the trees, that is, except the blank space where Frank was sitting with his empty pot of dirt.

The aging president noticed Frank right away. He called him to the front. The president questioned Frank on why his seed did not grow when everyone else was able to grow such beautiful lemon trees.

Frank responded "I tried, but I must confess, I was not able to grow the seed, no matter how hard I tried." Frank hung his head down and said "I am sorry".

The President looked at the pot of dirt and then looked at Frank. Then he said "Ladies and Gentlemen of the boardroom, I want to introduce you to your new president, Frank."

All was silent. *Was the old man off his rocker? Frank couldn't do one simple thing that was asked of him? What kind of president would he be if he could not handle one thing?*

The aging president continued. "One year ago today, I had handed everyone of you, one lemon seed, not a fertile lemon seed, but one made of *plastic*, incapable of growing anything!"

Disbelief and shame shown across all the gathered faces. You could hear a pin drop. The president continued "Frank was the only one who followed through with the original seed without compromising, he put *truth* in front of *desire*. The fruit I was hoping to produce was not lemons, but integrity. Thank you Frank, and congratulations."[xvii]

You will know the *truth* and the *truth* shall set you free. Just ask a farmer.

As the farmer waits for the land to yield its valuable crop, trusting God will send the rain and the sunshine, there is no place for short cuts, or cheating the integrity of the process. Harvest time will come. The farmer waits with hope, that God will make it rain, and the sun will shine, and the crops will come. The farmer learns to desire only what is the will of God, as the farmer partners with Him in the growing process. To fight it, is only fighting yourself. The farmer aligns himself with the will of God.

A young boy, excited about the taste of the apple he was eating, saved a seed and planted it in the cup of soil that he left in the window sill. He was so eager for his apple tree to grow that he worked every hour nurturing his seed, digging it up to check on it. Sure enough, after a couple of weeks, nothing ever happened and his impatience grew.

It wasn't until his grandfather told him that growing a seed is God's doing. Our job is to remain patient, tending to the needs of the seed from a distance. Nurturing the seed with life giving water, sunshine, and healthy soil; trusting that God is working his magic behind the scene, or under the soil.

Once the boy 'practiced' patience by trusting God's plan, sure enough, out of the soil, started the green shoot of what would eventually become an apple tree.

The apostle James said *"Be patient brothers and sisters...see how the farmer waits for the land to yield its valuable crop, patiently waiting for the autumn and spring rains."* [xviii]

At the Village, many of our residents remember growing up on the farm, and the planting of *Victory*

Gardens during the war. They also remember when food was not prevalent and they had to make do with what they could grow. It was a humbling time.

Many of our village residents share in the Community Supported Agriculture (CSA) project. Staff and residents alike participate in the labor of gardening together. The healthy produce that is produced, is shared on the salad bar in the dining room, where the whole community eats.

Continued work in the soil is a reminder of the partnership that we have with God and His provisions of soil, rain, sunshine, and seed. We become the vessels that prepare the ideal setting for God's provisions to produce our nourishment.

With time, patience and integrity, we hope for a plentiful harvest. The nutrition we get from fresh locally grown, organic vegetables is only part of the reward. The other is the work itself. The work becomes its own reward.

When one labors in a Community Supported Agriculture Garden, like we have at the village, the laborer receives a threefold blessing.

First with the harvest; secondly, with communion with God and neighbor through the labor; and third, the labor itself becomes the meaningful exercise of the day.

Combining the right ingredients of the elixir that the Creator provides: seed, soil, sunshine, and rain; we facilitate the growth of the food that sustains us. With our partnership with the Creator, we usher in the harvest. The harvest becomes so much more than fruits and vegetables. The harvest becomes a harmonious experience with the Creator, fortifying us spiritually and physically.

A seed, nestled in the soil, kissed by the sun, showered by the rain, blessed by God, produces the sustenance that provides life for all. What a partnership we have. God is good.

As stated in the Introduction, we can now restate the first of the three principles of health and wellness spelled out in this book. The first of the three principles is:

Everything we need for sustaining health and wellness had been provided for us through nature since the beginning. If not true, life would not be. Today's health crisis is not the fault of the individual, but is a manifestation of our community forgetting our blessings of real, whole, natural foods and simple life giving water.

The Principle of Meaningful Exercise

On any given day at the Village, you can see Charlie walking the perimeter of the 33 acre campus. A while back, we celebrated Charlie's one-hundredth birthday. It was a joyful occasion. Well wishers from all around the Village came to celebrate the next of several *Centarians* to have their home at the Village.

Nationally, a one-hundredth birthday, seems to be a very unique event, but not so much **at the Village**. We have many Centarians, with many more to come.

It is never a simple reason why so many folks stay so healthy for so long at the Village, but we can assume it has much to do with the three principles that have been spelled out in the introduction chapter. Certainly, we share the healthiest menu one can offer; and, we know that the strong sense of community has given new leases on all the lives in the Village. And, certainly the overall health of the Village has to do with the commitment to the exercise and movement that continues to be preached, not as a chore, but as an expression of gratitude and thanksgiving for life. It is felt campus wide, that when we *care for ourselves to better care for others*, our efforts made towards personal fitness becomes a true spiritual discipline. That motivation lasts a long lifetime.

Melissa Wallace, the Village's director of Wellness, can be found most mornings organizing or leading exercise classes and events that go beyond the one dimension of exercise simply to stay *physically* fit. Her vision surpasses exercising for the physical health of it. Her focus is the physical, but also, the social, mental, and the spiritual. She and her staff exercise the whole individual, and in so doing, she exercises the heart of the Village, by connecting together all the important aspects of a life. This multi-dimensional approach to wellness, makes all the difference.

It is the difference between counting calories and repetitions, to celebrating nutrient dense whole foods and enjoying meaningful purposeful activity. Exercise becomes so much more than a means of weight-loss.

In a time span where our food is getting more caloric, our inactive bodies are burning fewer calories. The combination has become disastrous for our the current health of the planet.

In addition to diet, it is precisely the *inactivity* of Americans that is linked directly to obesity, type 2 diabetes, heart disease, muscle atrophy, osteoporosis, hypertension, advancing arthritis, depression, certain cancers, and many other chronic conditions.

We know that moderate to heavy exercise improves all those conditions. When we exercise, or increase our activity in general, we improve our risk of falling victim to disabling chronic conditions that have become epidemic in America.

Obesity, type 2 diabetes, heart disease, muscle atrophy, osteoporosis, hypertension, advancing arthritis, and depression are responsible by and large for the bulk of the medical costs and prescriptions written for chronic conditions. But yet, we know that exercise can be a most effective force against the runaway usage of these medications.

At the Village, the true value of exercise is implied. Exercise improves all aspects of life. When we accept the gift of exercise, we accept abundant life. No longer are these chronic conditions the norm, but they become the exception.

Instead of chronic disease, anxiety, and depression; with exercise, the opposite happens: health and wellness. If we exercise consistently throughout life, we can truly slow or even reverse the aging process.

On a Sunday morning, a few of our *Centarians* make their way across the entire campus, walking completely independent. These Centarians are mobile and get to church under their own strength and efforts, largely due to their commitment to eating healthy, exercising regularly, and their devotion to their community of faith.

So this commitment to physical exercise can be expressed in the second principle that you read in the introduction. The first principle had to do with healthy foods. The second principle addresses the movement. It is as follows:

Unlike anything we create by hand, like a car or a refrigerator, which starts to breakdown when used; the body improves in every way with moderate to heavy use. Exercise is a magic pill, a fountain of youth, an anti-depressant; the body is improved in every way possible, naturally with exercise.

The Principle of Caring

There is a story of a woman, who was content in her life, even though she was poor. In her poverty, she would still always manage to have enough money to provide bread to travelers who had very little. She would load a loaf of bread in her bag on her morning trip to the river to wash clothes. She was very content and never lacked for anything, even though she appeared to have very little.

On one particular day, as she knelt down at the river to wash her clothes, she discovered a shiny stone at the bottom of the river where she washed. She picked it out of the water, and saw it was a precious rock, capable of providing more money than she would ever need. So she simply put it in her bag next to the bread and continued to wash, as she always did; whistling a tune while she worked, like she always did.

Soon a weary traveler came around and begged for a crust of bread, for he has been traveling long and had nothing to eat. She opened her bag and handed the loaf of bread to the traveler. The traveler spotted the stone. After eating the bread together, the traveler told of *his* story of being a terribly poor and asked the woman if he might be able to have her precious stone. The woman thought nothing of it and said of course, I already have what I need. The man eagerly reached for the stone.

The next day, as the woman was washing at the same familiar spot, whistling her familiar tune, as she always did, the weary traveler returned for a second visit.

He held out the stone to give it back to the woman and said "I hope you do not mind, but I would like you to have this back in exchange of something much more valuable than it is worth. Please share with me what allows you to *not* hold onto something so valuable as that stone. Surely what you possess is worth much more than money."

The woman gladly shared with the beggar, where to find the bread that will always satisfy. For she had placed in her heart the knowing of God's love and the love of neighbor.

Love is the most precious of stones.

Every night **at the Village**, Del, one of the residents, entertains at the piano in the elevator lobby. For years she volunteers playing for a crowd of neighbors. She plays for the sheer joy of sharing her music that is inside her, that so naturally flows outward for the benefit of the Village.

One of the neighbors who enjoyed her music nightly was Richard, who was 96 years of age when he passed away. His apartment was as close as you can get to the lobby where Del played her piano every night.

Listening to her music became a favorite thing for Richard to do. Yet, in the last days, he was unable to get out of bed to come listen to the nightly concert. Because of the position of his bedroom wall, he could not hear the music as it was being played in the piano lobby. Not only could Richard not get out of bed, but he could not hear the beautiful music he enjoyed so much.

Julia, Richard's wife, decided she would like to have a digital piano for her husband to listen to, because he enjoyed the music so much.

Cheryl, the Foundation Director at the Village, offered to run out to pick-up the digital piano keyboard at the local music store. Cheryl sensed an urgency to pick up the piano, because of Richard's failing physical condition. So, to follow through with Julia's wish for her husband, Cheryl went to the music store, picked up the digital piano, and set it up in Richard's room all within a few hours.

That same evening, Del came in to play for him after her nightly concert was finished in the lobby. She played his favorite numbers, covering all the songs he loved so much.

When Del finished the set, Richard clapped his hands together, and said his last audible word, this side of heaven. He said "beautiful".

Ninety minutes later, Richard took his last breath and made his journey from this world to the next.

The digital keyboard was dedicated to the Village at the memorial service of Dr. Richard Rush.

The *physical* gift was the digital keyboard; but the *spiritual* gift is the compassionate journey it took to finally arrive at the Village. It was purchased by a loving wife, delivered by a caring employee, and played by a committed neighbor for Richard on his last hours of life, this side of heaven.

Each and every time the community uses that digital piano, we remember its roots; and the music that comes from it, will always be used as a *gift* to the neighbor. The digital keyboard story will continue to spread *Village magic* each time it plays.

When we choose to eat what has been provided for us naturally; whole and healthy foods from the soil, the trees and the vine; when we choose to stay *well* through participating in the gift of meaningful exercise; and when we choose to *care for ourselves to better care for others*, we are a living example of *aging grace*.

This is the heart and health of any community.

When you re-examine deeper the place you currently reside and the community of people whom you currently rely; you will discover that the order of the life you live is far from random chance.

You have discovered our *Thin Place* at the Village, now explore yours. Live with the awareness that your life is part of a God blessed miracle. Then you will understand fully the three variables needed for a lifetime of excellent health and wellness: *a healthy diet, meaningful exercise, and...an abundant awareness of the Creator's love.*

So finally, we arrive at our third and final principle that rounds out the message of this book. In a *Thin Place*, where the physical and the spiritual are close at hand, it makes sense that:

When we care for ourselves to better care for others, our efforts made towards personal fitness becomes a true spiritual discipline; an expression of gratitude and thanksgiving for all of life.

*****

Endotes

[i] Manning, Brennan *All is Grace (Colorado Springs: David Cook,. 2011) pg. 33*

[ii] I Corinthians 13:1-13.

[iii] Williamson, Marianne (New York: HarperCollins, 1993) pg. 191

[iv] Luke 16: 19-31

[v] *The Fiery Sermon*, author unknown.

[vi] *Little Girls Shoes*, author Unknown.

[vii] Silverstein, Shel *The Giving Tree* (New York: Harper & Row, 1964).

[viii] John 21:15-17.

[ix] Keith, Kent *The Paradoxical Commandments* (Navato, Ca., New World Library, 2003).

[x] Luke 15:11-32.

[xi] Hughes, Tim *Here I am To Worship*, 1999.

[xii] Wallis, Jim *God's Politics* (New York: HarperCollins, 2005), pg. 35

[xiii] Campolo, Tony *Let Me Tell You a Story* (Nashville: Thomas Nelson, 2000) Pg. 164.

[xiv] Tolle, Eckhart *The Power of Now* (Vancouver, B.C.:Namaste Publishing, 1999) pg. 11.

[xv] Adapted from The Grimm's Fairy Tales, #78, *The Old Grandfather and His Grandson*.

[xvi] Luke 7:36-50.

[xvii] Adapted from *The Emporer's Seed*, Author Unknown.

[xviii] James 5:7, HOLY BIBLE, NIV (1984).

Other Books by Tom Hafer

Wellplanet: Fitness as a Spiritual Discipline
Before becoming a monk, Brother Mark O'Reilly was an extraordinary small town physician. With his guru-like clarity, this 88 year old sage introduces Fitness as a Spiritual Discipline to his student, Hope. His timeless wisdom is for everyone who has fought the demons of weight-loss and won, then lost, then gained, then lost. For the sake of our personal health, our neighbor, and the planet; we have never had a timelier message to embrace...once again.

Worzalla Publishing, 2010 (www.tomhafer.com)

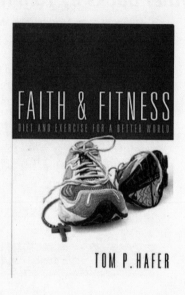

Faith & Fitness: Diet and Exercise for a Better World
Faith & Fitness orchestrates the integration of the Physical, Spiritual and the Environmental aspects of our lives; creating a deeper understanding of the Creator's intention for the health of all His people and the planet. It is the way we grow, eat, and share food that cures obesity and world hunger. It is the way we see exercise; no longer is it a necessary chore, it is reclaimed as the beautiful physical healing gift it was intended to be.

Augsburg Books bestseller, 2007 (www.tomhafer.com)

Acclaim for Faith & Fitness

"Faith and Fitness contains within its pages sound theological foundation for holistic health." *(Circuit Rider) The United Methodist Church*

Filled with practical ideas about food, exercise, and total wellness, the book explores the connections between real and spiritual sustenance, affluence, and exercise and the relationship between a healthy congregation and healthy individuals.
Evangelical Lutheran Church in America (Seeds for the Parish)

"'Faith and Fitness' literally changed my life!" *Chaplain, Hickman Air Force Base*

"Rev. Hafer offers weight-loss salvation through God." **E! Entertainment Television**

"This hippie-preacher who is more U2's Bono than Billy Graham says the real focus should be consuming the right amount of food ourselves and saving the excess resources for the millions dying of hunger." *USA Today*

"This book is for all Christians who have a deep concern for social justice, advocates better self-care for the purpose of caring for others and the planet"
Publisher's weekly

"An abundance of wisdom and helpful advice on the topics of nutrition and exercise."
The Catholic Review

For someone like me whose life motto is "faith, family, fitness," this book is a must-read
Les Steckel, former NFL coach, author and President, Fellowship of Christian Athletes, Kansas, MO

About the Author, Rev. Tom Hafer

Tom is pictured here at the Village with some of the
Centarians (100 year olds): Phyllis, Miriam, Charlie, Alice, and Fran.
Photo by www.melindahawkins.com

Books

Faith & Fitness: *Diet and Exercise for a Better World*
(Augsburg Books, 2007, *Bestseller*).

Wellplanet: *Fitness as a Spiritual Discipline*
(Worzalla Publishing, 2010).

 Aging Grace: The Journey to a Healthy 100
(Worzalla Publishing, 2012).

The Trilogy reflect the principle:

When we care for ourselves to better care for others, our efforts made towards personal fitness becomes a true spiritual discipline; an expression of gratitude and thanksgiving for all of life.

Faith & Fitness is a nonfiction link between our physical and spiritual lives, for a clearer vision of our personal and global health.

Wellplanet is the easy to read fiction novel, as told by the wisdom of the ages.

And, **Aging Grace** is the true story of a Village that practices the principles for wellness: a healthy diet, meaningful exercise, and an abundant awareness of the Creator's love.

Tom is a Physical Therapist and an ordained Pastor. He currently serves at Gulf Coast Village (The Village) as Chaplain and Physical Therapist in Cape Coral, Florida. He travels and speaks on the topic of *Faith & Fitness*.

www.tomhafer.com

GULF COAST
VILLAGE

A Family of Senior Living Options

This is the **Village**, in real life. The *Thin Place*, in which this book got its inspiration. It is one of the 400 communities of Volunteers of America and is in Cape Coral, Florida. *Gulf Coast Village* is a Family of Senior Living Options that allows older Americans to maintain their independence and quality of life regardless of their current level of dependence. For more than twenty years, the focus of Gulf Coast Village Retirement Community has been to improve the quality of life for seniors in our community and provide the best health care possible. The Gulf Coast Village Foundation is a non-profit organization providing a philanthropic vehicle to encourage financial support for the development of programs that meet the diverse needs of older adults. At the Village, we can provide everything from an occasional helping hand to full-time care. Our work touches the mind, body, heart — and ultimately the spirit — of those we served by integrating our deep compassion with highly effective programs and services for our residents, families, and the greater community we serve.

www.GulfCoastVillage.com

Senior Choice at Home by Gulf Coast Village is a unique membership–based program that offers comprehensive health care and personal assistance at home. This program is for older adults who must qualify while they are healthy and independent, offering financial security and peace of mind. If healthy senior living and being independent at home are important to you or a loved one, contact us today for more information.

Geri Spaeth, *Executive Director of Senior Choice at Home*
www.seniorchoiceathome.com

Volunteers of America®

There are no limits to caring.®

Volunteers of America is a national, nonprofit, faith-based organization dedicated to helping those in need live healthy, safe, and productive lives. Since 1896, our ministry of service has supported and empowered America's most vulnerable group, including: the frail elderly, people with disabilities, at-risk youth, men and women returning from prison, homeless individuals and families, those recovering from addictions, and many others. Through hundreds of human service programs including housing and health care; Volunteers of America helps more than 2 million people in over 400 communities. We offer a variety of services for older Americans, in particular, that allow them to maintain their independence and quality of life – everything from an occasional helping hand to full-time care. Our work touches the mind, body, heart — and ultimately the spirit — of those we serve by integrating our deep compassion with highly effective programs and services.

AGING WITH OPTIONS™

As one of the largest nonprofit providers of affordable senior housing in the United States, as well as a leading nonprofit provider of skilled nursing care and assisted living, Volunteers of America believes our mission today is to rise to the challenge of caring for an aging America.

With today's advancements in health care and special emphasis on preventive care; older Americans are experiencing a future of better health and longevity. No matter what stage of aging, no matter what state of health, Volunteers of America can offer the right support at the right time. We have the expertise to coordinate all the care and support necessary to meet each individual's needs, helping people maintain independence and self-sufficiency.

Building upon our long-established and trusted services for seniors, Aging with Options™ provides choices and support through each phase of life's journey. We do this through community engagement-home, community-based services, and the PACE

(Program of All-inclusive Care for the Elderly) model of care management.

Volunteers of America invites everyone into its circle of caring and supports every older adult's right to age in place-surrounded by family and friends.

www.VolunteersofAmerica.org.